How To Change Your Mindset in 30 Days

Positive Thinking & Behaviour for Success

By Leon Lyons

MindsetMastership.com

About the Author

Leon Lyons is a senior coach at Mindset Mastership, a life coaching business based in London, England.

Mindset Mastership teaches clients how human behaviour really works. Through our teaching we have helped worldwide clients gain a better advantage, to develop themselves and achieve more from life.

For further details, see:
MindsetMastership.com

Table of Contents

Introduction 1

    Bonus Hack - 30 day Mindset Change 1 3

    Bonus Hack - 30 Day Mindset Change 2 4

    Bonus Hack - 30 day Mindset Change 3........................4

Chapter 1: Positive Thinking/ Mindset – An Introduction 6

    1.1 Introduction 6

    1.2 How to Apply Positive Thinking...............................6

    1.3 The Traits of a Positive Mindset 10

    1.4 Positive Attitude is the Key to Success 12

    1.5 Positive mindset and Leadership.............................27

Chapter 2: Ways to Achieve Positive Mindset 29

    2.1. Help Students Develop a Positive Mindset for a Positive Attitude...32

    2.2. Games and Activities to Teach Positive Mindset Skills.. 34

Chapter 3: Positive Thinking Techniques to Gain Achievements 57

    Fixed Vs Growth Mindset 60

    FIXED MINDSET 62

    GROWTH MINDSET... 62

Chapter 4: To Gain Achievements, Success is Mandatory...88

    4.1. Techniques of Success.................................... 88

    4.2. How to Make Your Day Productive......................... 91

    4.3. The Initiation of Success 93

Chapter 5: Factors Governing Mindset 94

    5.1. Law of Attraction....................................... 94

    5.2. Have Faith in your Creative Power 96

    5.3. Your Unlimited Power.................................... 96

Chapter 6: Know the Truth about Yourself 98

    6.1. Ego... 99

6.2. You Create Yourself 99

6.3. Never Belittle Yourself 100

6.4. Self-Acceptance is Freedom..................................101

6.5. How you Treat Yourself Forms the Basis of your Mindset.. 102

Chapter 7: Self-Discovery 104

7.1. Change your World 106

7.2. Identify your Goals 108

7.3. Your Attitude Affects your Success...................... 109

7.4. Never Force Change – That is failure 111

Chapter 8: Seeing is Believing 113

8.1. Success Suffers a Setback due to Perception of Reality...113

8.2. Focusing on the End Result 115

8.3. Think Outside your Limitations 115

8.4. What We Think, We Attract...................................116

Chapter 9: Create your Own Story 117

9.1. Is your life about Problems or Solutions?.............117

Chapter 10: Success, Mindset and Law of Attraction 121

10.1. Manifesting Success Using the Law of Attraction 123

10.2. Achieve your Financial Desires........................... 124

10.3. Create Wealth with Imagination......................... 126

10.4. Be grateful – that's Being Positive 127

Chapter 11: Words that Create Results at a Faster Pace.. 128

11.1. Your Conscious Mind Creates Result................... 128

Chapter 12: Think Positive, Identify Your Problems and Achieve Success 131

12.1. Identify the Problem and its Solution to Bring about the Change 131

12.2. Self-reliance over Emotional Dependency 132

12.3. Say No to Fear of Uncertainty 135

12.4. Staying Focused, Knowing your Desire – Path of Success..135

12.5. Say No to Fear of Change....................................136

12.6. Difference between Successful and Unsuccessful People 137

Chapter 13: The Amazing 7 Growth Hacks........ 139

Hack 1 - Become Aware Of Your Thoughts..................139

Hack 2 - Reframe Your Thoughts Using The Ctfar Model
....140

Hack 3 - Positive Affirmations 141

Hack 4 - Get Rid Of Limiting Words...........................141

Hack 5 - Ask Yourself Questions 142

Hack 6 - Add "No Matter What" To Your Thought Process..142

Hack 7 - Create An Alter Ego For Yourself 143

Conclusion..145

References...147

Introduction

The truth is, none of us can wake up and remarkably change our lives other than ourselves.

Studies have shown that 80% of our daily thoughts are negative self-talk. This means unfiltered thoughts enter our minds leaving us with harmful emotions. We must find better solutions in controlling negative mindsets to help us turn our lives around.

We use powerful mindset change methods such as CTFAR & the 5 R's: these approaches will reprogram the way you think – AND build a stronger, more positive mind.

The Seven-Step plan is easy, simple, clear and a little fun. The first few days we'll begin with small activities, and then we will gradually build up to more significant changes that you can experiment. Throw away any mistakes you may have had and start fresh the next day. Trying to connect with meaningful experiences gives you a jolt of inspiration. We are guided by how things make us feel. With your goals floating around in your mind, let them simmer a little bit while we create a living space.

This begins with one enormous clean-up. We use minimalism and create space to help purify your daily thoughts. We all have one room where we sit down and do some tasks. These tasks could include reading, browsing the internet, writing, doing business, etc. Change that space and it will do something that will click inside you, giving you pleasure and happiness. Throw out all that doesn't make you happy or makes you feel bad (feelings are head and centre again). There are a lot of distractions that keep us from diving into our goals.

Go through your calendar with a fine-tooth comb. You'll notice how frequently you are side-tracked and wasting your time. The approach I want you to take is as follows:

- Don't get offended by people's opinions anymore.
- Stop the game of comparison and live your own life.
- Be YOU at home and at work. Take the mask off.
- Stop thinking all the time and just follow your intuition.

It will be almost too easy that your mind can decide to opt-out and reframe a mindset. Often, the best recommendation is the simplest, and it's the little stuff you don't do that restrains you from having the transformation you've always wanted— and definitely need.

The following mindset change hacks are an extra bonus, which when accompanied with the 7 hacks mentioned at the end of the book are a powerful source. You will need to read the whole book - or if listening to the audio, listen to it in its entirety to gain the full value.

Bonus Hack - 30 day Mindset Change 1

Get an empty small glass jar – you want to be able to see what's inside and have it within easy reach. Every day you will write a short note, word, or sentence and place it in the jar. It needs to be a positive, progressive thought to encourage you to stay on track with your: diet, business plan, gym routine, office work, new career, exam revision or any or personal goals.

It could be any of the following;

    Day 1   - Excited and looking forward to tomorrow.
    Day 2   - Easy Peasy!
    Day 23 - Still loving it!
    Day 24 - Committed!
    Day 25 - I love reading.

Every day you will add another small slip of paper with a positive note. At the end of each month, you will look back at all the notes and reflect how far you have come. The goal is more about the journey and less about the destination.

Bonus Hack - 30 Day Mindset Change 2

Find a calendar with enough space to write a short word or sentence under each day and place it on your wall. Every night before you get ready for bed, reflect on the day that has come to an end and write about it on the calendar.

Alternatively, create a morning routine and produce a form of gratitude and thanks for the day ahead. This motivates you to keep progressing along as well as encouraging you to continue taking action in your daily life.

As you visibly see the calendar on your wall, you will notice how your daily goals are manifesting tangible change into your life. Recording this is a way to recognise that change is happening, especially when it is often difficult to feel a difference.

Bonus Hack - 30 day Mindset Change 3

Choose 1 day each month where you do nothing but provide yourself a day of self-care. I suggest going to a local spa, or a gym with spa facilities such as: a swimming pool, Jacuzzi, steam room and sauna. Perhaps go for a haircut at your favourite salon or get a beard trim from the coolest barber in your city. Treat yourself to a pedicure, or a relaxing day in the park. Read a book and have a nice meal. This serves two benefits. First, you get to relax and enjoy a full day of small, self-indulgence; and second, you can reward yourself for staying on track with your goals and behaviour changes. This can help you associate hard work with a little bit of play.

Chapter 1: Positive Thinking/ Mindset –
An Introduction

"Don't be pushed around by the fears in your mind. Be led by the dreams in your heart." - Roy T. Bennett

---

1.1 Introduction

Positive thinking is a mental attitude where positive results are expected. Increasingly, courses and books about this concept are attracting more people. More and more successful people say that they achieve what they want because of their optimistic lifestyle. A person with a positive attitude - both professionally and socially - will always be more successful than a person who doesn't have control of his or her thoughts.

1.2 How to Apply Positive Thinking

It is not easy to change everything that you've learned in life. Immediately implementing positive thinking isn't that easy, but over time, you will get results. Use meaningful words when you speak. Instead of telling yourself "I can't," persuade yourself that you will do all you can.

For example, tell yourself:
- "I will do all I can to have a good friendship."
- "I will do all I can to have a brilliant career."
- "I will do all I can to keep myself safe."

Delete all negative feelings: If you are in a bad mood, do not let negative thoughts and feelings prevail. Eradicate stress each day by focusing on good things in your life.

Use terms that are powerful and successful: Fill your thoughts with words that make you feel powerful, happy and guided in the right direction.

Practice positive statements: Positive self-talk is one of the most common practices of positive thinking. Repeat a meaningful expression or mantra, like "I deserve to be happy," or "I deserve to be cherished." The more it's repeated, the more your brain changes to make it feel true.

Redirect your feelings and thoughts: A common method of psychotherapists is to redirect your thoughts in situations where you feel bad. To create a happier mindset, think of a positive image that you can go back to whenever your thoughts need to be redirected.

Start thinking positively and then you'll succeed: Nothing compares to self-confidence, which often leads to success. Put aside your fears and trust that your goals will be accomplished when you start thinking positively.

Examine what goes wrong: Though we stress that it's important to stay positive, being in complete denial is not a positive approach. If something goes wrong, take some time to identify the problem, discover what led to the current situation, and create a plan to avoid future mistakes. Just do not dwell on the problem for too long.

Please pardon yourself: If you continuously fight about things that go wrong, nothing will change. Tell yourself that you are forgiven, and you can continue.

Give failure a chance: Even the worst experiences in our lives can give us new, positive opportunities. For example, after losing your job, you might be able to start your own business or go back in school!

Based on your imagination: It can be a great motivation to imagine what you want to do, the ideal personality you want to have, and how to make it come to fruition!

Positivity doesn't always mean smiling and looking happy, it's more about your general outlook on life and your desire to concentrate on all that's good in life.

Accommodating Negative Thoughts and Negative emotions

According to psychologist Barbara Fredrickson, you should concentrate on risks, threats and vulnerabilities. This was important for the survival of our ancestors, after all.

Positive thoughts and feelings, on the other hand, "expand and create" our tools and abilities, and open up more possibilities for us (Fredrickson 2004).

You do not need to be annoyingly optimistic when building the foundation for your positive thoughts, but rather have trust in yourself and your future. It is all right to feel pessimistic, but in the long run, choosing to respond with hope, confidence and gratitude will help you much more.

Apart from developing your skills and personal resources, there are many other advantages to maintaining a positive attitude - including improving overall well-being and building stronger stress management capabilities. According to experts in the Mayo Clinic, positive thinking will enhance your life, minimize depression and stress levels, give you more immunity to the common cold, improve your overall psychological and physical well-being, boost your cardiovascular health and protect you from cardiovascular disease.

Benefits of Positive Mindset and Attitude at your Workplace

Nothing captures a positive attitude in the workplace more than Psychological Capital (PsyCap). This multi-component framework is composed of four psychological resources. Luthans and Youssef in 2004, renowned management and leadership researchers, created the positive and developmental states of an individual, the four characteristics being: Hope, Efficacy, Resilience & Optimism, known shorter as the PsyCap, is a "positive psychological asset." Their theory quickly spread amongst supportive therapists in the institutions, and by 2011, hundreds of PsyCap references were already written.

The Four 'PsyCap Positive 'components:

Hope – Where motivation & power to take action in goal planning intersect.
Efficacy – Ones own belief in confidence to achieve specific goals
Resilience – The ability to overcome adversity, stress, conflict, failure and change
Optimism – Not fixed to negative events, but optimism reinforces efficacy and hope

The first formal study of PsyCap was conducted in 2011, and it highlighted several of PsyCap's many advantages at work. PsyCap was positively related to job satisfaction, organisational engagement and emotional well-being.

HOPE

Hope and positivity are personality traits closely linked to physiological and psychological well- being.

Hope is a cognitive process. It motivates a person to find the will and the ways and means that lead to positive emotions. And it certainly doesn't mean donning an unrealistic hope that everything will turn out fine.

Here's why…

Hope can be viewed as a process consisting of three components.

1. Goals
2. Pathways
3. Agency

Professor Snyder discovered that hopeful people are those who see many pathways to goals because they anticipate obstacles. Hopeful people, according to this theory, don't expect the journey to be easy.

How does one hope? How do you put hope into practice?
First, decide on the goal you want to work on. Your goal must be something you care about.
It must be specific and measurable.

It must also have a deadline.

Write it down. Contemplate on how it would feel to reach this goal.

Second, develop a pathway. How will you reach your goal? Often enough, your goal will consist of subgoals.

Develop a variety. Do you have a plan A? Plan B? C? D?

Hopeful people ANTICIPATE obstacles and know that the process won't always be easy-peasy. When people visualise obstacles, they make concrete plans. And when you make concrete plans, you are more likely to reach your goals.

Having alternative plans not only ensures success, it also allows you more energy. This is because you know that a setback is just a delay. It won't stop you from achieving your goals, nor would it demoralise you.

Also, discern if you are trying to overcome an obstacle. Most of the time, people merely need to "pummel through". In that case, you must factor in mental and physical exhaustion, as well.

difficulty for what they are may be a better step to take to endure for the meantime.

2. Searching for Meaning

Resilience is finding meaning and purpose when faced with a situation that cannot be altered. A lot of energy is spent fearing what cannot be controlled. Ask, what is this roadblock teaching me? What can I do better next time? Be of the mindset that this setback's lesson is preparatory for something even bigger and more significant.

3. Learning How to Improvise

Your ability to bounce back can be gleaned from the way with which you face a situation with whatever you have at the moment. It isn't so much the tools or the resources you have. It's the ability to create new ways to reach a goal. The best leaders are masters at this.

OPTIMISM

Optimism is all about acknowledging the likelihood of success now and in the future. Optimists believe that good things will happen to them – regardless of their situation.

To develop optimism, you must change your focus. This can be done by acknowledging and accepting the past, appreciating the present, and seeing the future as a place of opportunity. Why all this focus on the "past"? The answer lies in perspective. When you change your perception of the past, you affect how you see the impact it has on the future. Coaches use "reframing" as a technique in coaching and therapy sessions. The past cannot be changed, but it can be used as a stepping stone for future plans.

Furthermore, optimism is a smorgasbord of positive responses. You cannot control your initial reaction. But you certainly can control your RESPONSE.

For instance, angry frustration from rejection is a reaction.

But you can change your response by keeping in mind how even the most negative settings have a silver lining. (There could be a better opportunity waiting in line!)

Practice gratitude despite the negativity because everything is a learning experience. Toxic work culture? Surround yourself with positive people. Remember that even the good life has its downs. Psychological Capital is closely linked to wellbeing, work, satisfaction, and happiness. Developing just one in the HERO pillars (hope, efficacy, resilience, and optimism) already positively impacts employees / members.

1.5 Positive mindset and Leadership

Just as a positive attitude is vital to rank and file, it is easy to understand why leaders need a positive attitude as well. Experts Hannah, Woolfolk and Lord (2009) proposed a model for effective leadership based on the idea of "the right thing" being able to bring people together with a good sense of self-improvement. In this concept, a leader with a positive attitude is more likely to be better performing and more involved. Through role modelling and social influence, they are also better suited for leading others to have a more positive attitude.

Another set of research conducted at the same time confirmed the relationship between the leader and the followers; management trust affected PsyCap positively and had a major impact on leaders' and followers' success.

Management trust is also related to successful leadership and achievement. Although faith in management does not necessarily indicate that both leaders and supporters have a positive mindset, it benefits to have a positive workplace attitude.

Forbes author Victor Lipman (2017) puts observations like this in simpler terms: "You can always pursue someone with a positive mindset more easily." This means that a leader's positive attitude is going to attract followers and inspire encouragement and dedication in their subordinates.

Leaders have to be constantly "on" and spend a great deal of their time as a solid, confident leader. This job is tiring; it will enable leaders to remain positive and resilient in difficult situations.

Chapter 2: Ways to Achieve Positive Mindset

"A Positive mind always considers and so realise that even failure is a part of success." - Manna Sangma

In this chapter, we show you some of the most popular and proven methods to achieve a positive mindset. Larry Alton (Success.com) has shared some practical tips to help someone get motivated. Here are a few of his tips:

- Start the day with positive statements.

- Concentrate on good things; no matter how small they are.

- Even in bad situations, find humour.

- Transform shortcomings into lessons and learn from them!

- Convert negative self-speaking into some positive self-speaking.

- Concentrate on the present rather than dwelling in the past or losing yourself in the future.

- Ask friends, colleagues, family, contacts and networks to help and encourage you to find supportive peers, mentors and colleagues.

Brian Tracy, who is a successful author and speaker, adds a few more tips in this regard. According to him, you should:

- Remember that your response determines the outcome of a situation.

- Chase down negative thoughts, using positive affirmations or phrases.

- Include motivational and optimistic statements in your life.

- Be pleased, thankful and carry on the best of intentions for the people around.

- Challenge yourself if something goes wrong.

- Show the world how strong and optimistic you are!

One should also consider some of the tips from Megan Wycklendt, which she stated in Fulfillment Daily Newspaper. According to her:

- One should take their problems as a growth opportunity.

- It is great to be rejected. Rejection happens to everyone!

- To characterise life, one should use positive words.

- Replace what you will have with what you already have.

- Don't indulge yourself into the problems of others.

- Breathe! Intentionally, consciously and attentively.

- In times of tragedy and violence, remember that the right and good will happen.

- Utilise positive approach to overcome difficulties.

- Make others smile.

Moving forward, Dr Tchiki Davis's strategies can also motivate you to attain a positive attitude. You just have to ask yourself, "Do I really think positively?".

We have a checklist for you to do your own analysis so that you may examine where you are standing.

- Do you reinforce your positive thoughts by using positive words?

- Do you reinforce your brain's ability to deal with information using a positive approach?

- Do you enhance the ability of your brain to focus on the positive things in your daily routine?

- Do you practise appreciation?

- Do you try to savour every good moment?

2.1. Help Students Develop a Positive Mindset for a Positive Attitude

You can encourage students to try the above techniques and pass on the benefits of developing a positive mentality. However, there are some other ways students can become more efficient in improving their attitude towards education and school.

Elliot Seif, a well-known writer, discusses thirteen ways in which students can increase their concern about their education.

1. Build the element of hope among students. This allows students to understand the importance of working hard and provides them with more chances to focus on their areas of interest.

2. Include positive information regarding their strengths on their daily, weekly and annual reports. Criticize them less!

3. Make them think instead of relying on textbooks.

4. Focus on the strengths of students instead of their weaknesses. Help them see that "the glass is half-full" rather than "the glass is half-empty." Understand that not all students are strong in every area. Encourage them to explore their strengths and interests. Teach students that they should see failure as a learning opportunity. This will surely encourage them to refine and improve their work.

5. Encourage them to slow down the process of reading and focus on what they consider to be relevant.

6. Tell students to concentrate on lessons and subjects that help them develop skills.

7. Encourage students to ask and answer questions. They are fundamental to their learning environment and their school's culture.

8. Write clear explanations for key issues. In case directions weren't clear, let students

know that no question is too little or too dumb to ask.

9. Provide students with several after-school programs. This will allow students to build and expand their interests.

10. Use survey teaching methods.

11. Consider taking learning interactions as far as possible.

12. Create more ways to integrate student interest in a subject. For example, you may wear all red (to represent communism) while delivering a lecture on a revolution.

13. Help students create paths for success. For this, you may take your students on field trips.

2.2. Games and Activities to Teach Positive Mindset Skills

If you are interested in some realistic ways of enhancing your positive attitude, you are in the right place! You can use various exercises to improve your positive thinking. Some of the best known are mentioned here!

•   Music may place you in a positive state of mind, so take advantage of it.

- Express your gratitude and appreciation for everyone and everything good in your life. Write down your gratitude so that you remember. Literally, write them down!

- Get some air! It profoundly affects your mind - slowly but surely - and steers it back to an optimistic and peaceful place.

- Don't let people label you. You are far more than a label.

- Don't question your inner confidence.

- Engage in positive activities, such as meditation, yoga, biking, athletics or whatever you enjoy.

- Stay in control and try to change any bad thoughts that come to mind.

- Don't move too quickly or push yourself too hard; everybody struggles, and that doesn't mean you're not good enough.

- Pay attention to what you eat and make sure to choose a healthy and optimistic diet.

- Change yourself! Whether or not you want it, it's better to embrace positive change.

Moving forward, if you're more interested in some fun, play the following games so that you improve your thoughts.

The Glad Game

Have you ever lost a job or split up with a partner, only to dwell on negative thoughts about the incident?

In this game, first introduced by the Disney movie Pollyanna, the main character consciously cultivates positive thinking. The other players are encouraged to turn the feelings of the first person into constructive ones; for example, they can say something like, "Now that I've lost my job, I'm going to have more time for my side business." This game encourages you to find the silver lining amongst the dark clouds and look for possibilities instead of despair.

Egg Balancing Game

The balanced egg game can be challenging, but an essential lesson in constructive thinking and open-mindedness.

Set a raw egg onto a slightly textured tabletop for your players (use a tablecloth). Ask them to figure out a way to make the egg sit tall on the tabletop. You may think it's unlikely to happen, but you can guarantee that it will happen soon! Let them try for a while. It may work, but in the end, you will probably need to give them a little mound of salt to balance the egg. This is an important thing to remember - when you think outside the box, things that seem unlikely are often possible.

Hunt for Happiness

Have the players mention things that make their lives worth living or things that make them happy. Once everyone has a list ready, send them on a scavenger hunt to collect as many items as possible on the list. You can set your mark. You'll have to be creative to check off everything on the list, particularly abstract stuff like "love." In addition to your positive thinking, it will also motivate you to improve your creative thinking. More games and events are available to help kids develop a positive attitude. Give those activities a try if you are a teacher, mother, coach or anyone who communicates with children.

Positive Steps Towards Well-Being

You can interactively show what you have done or want to try by taking notes. You may boost your well-being by:

- Taking on a hobby or developing a new skill.
- Doing some work and helping other people relax.
- Maintaining a healthy balance between sleep and work.

2.3 Positive Thinking Methods

<u>For Kids</u>

It's a tough time to be a kid these days. Mental health issues previously within the exclusive domain of adults are now as much a concern for kids.

How does one prepare a child to face such negativity? How do you equip young children to better deal with peer pressure, frustration, as well as all sorts of negative emotions?

The quick answer lies in building up their confidence. A confident child is a child poised for success, good health, and happiness. They are most likely to bounce back from setbacks quickly and won't hesitate to seek the help of a trusted adult.

The key is YOU. Parents, guardians, and teachers play a pivotal role in building a young child's confidence and self-assurance.

Some effective strategies that you may want to incorporate are as follows:

1. <u>Make sure they know that you love them unconditionally</u>.

    How they perceive what you feel or think of them has an intense bearing on the way they see

For those who work in the academe, you may want to tweak your classroom by:

- Keeping grades private
- Avoiding groupings according to ability
- Acknowledging small successes
- Providing opportunities to redo homework

5. Encourage acts of kindness.

Have your teen do something special for themselves and another person each day. This helps them think positively as it gives them something to look forward to daily.

6. Encourage gratitude

A daily journal to record the positive things that happened to them that day is a great way to grow a positive mindset. We tend to look at situations differently when times are rough. But if we have reminders of how things have been going right for us, then perhaps, life isn't as bad as it seems after all.

7. Encourage a part-time job.

This is a practical way to help build self-confidence, understand the world, develop early stages of working life, and also begin the practice of money management.

For Parents

There are books, videos, talks, blogs, conferences, and seminars on parenting abound. But nothing ever prepares you for parenthood and all the worrying that comes with it.

It seems that parenthood and worry will always be in the same sentence. Parents worry about their children's health and welfare. Is he safe? How will this affect my marriage? My career? Am I giving my daughter enough time? Should I have forced myself to breastfeed? Should one of us stay home? Does this cough merit a trip to the doctor? My child is on the autism spectrum, will he be ok? How do I shield my child from bullying and substance abuse? The list is endless.

As a soon-to-be parent, new parent, or future parent, know that you aren't the only one grappling with these fears. Here are some of the more common fears and how to calm them.

1. *"I know I'll just end up hurting my baby!"* – Newborns are delicate, but they aren't teacups. The possibility of dropping your baby or giving him too much medicine is highly unlikely. Just as you'd prepare for an office presentation, knowledge is power, and practice makes perfect. If you're iffy or feeling uncertain about something, call your paediatrician. They've heard it all. Further, success favours the prepared. Seek

For Men

Men won't admit it, but a lot of them suffer from anxieties too. It's different for everyone but the most common risk factors for men developing anxiety or depression include:

- A significant change in civil status or living arrangements (separation, divorce, death of a spouse)
- Physical health issues
- Relationship problems
- Loss of work
- Issues at the place of work
- Pregnancy and birth of a baby
- Drug and alcohol use
- Bullying

Among all these issues, work and the workplace seem to have the most significant impact on the mental health of males. Factors that contribute to job-related anxieties include high demands, work pressure, overload, an unclear work role, job insecurity, long working hours, bullying, and low job control. Physical signs of anxiety may include restlessness, panic attacks, insomnia, shortness of breath, a racing heart, muscle tension, and even vertigo.

The most important thing for men to know is anxiety and depression are not weaknesses.

An action plan for anxiety can cover a wide range of choices. Include exercise and stress management. Make sleep an "appointment" and not something to forego. Talk to a medical practitioner. These are real mental issues and not something you "get" because you aren't strong enough.

Try to include activities and hobbies that you enjoy. Look after your body by eating healthy, staying active, and getting plenty of sleep. Avoid drugs and alcohol – even if it helps you block the negative feelings in the meantime.

If you are supporting someone with anxiety, here are ways for you to help them:

- Listen without judgment. Let them know that you're there to listen without being judgmental.
- Offer to go with them to doctor's appointments.
- Encourage them to get enough sleep and exercise.
- Don't pressure them into participating in activities. Instead, encourage them to go out and spend time with family and friends.
- Have a doctor and hospital number ready just in case you notice that they become a threat to others or themselves. Numbers that you should have handy include a GP's, a psychologist, a psychiatrist, and a suicide hotline.

Avoid giving them more anxiety by telling them to "snap out of it". (If they could, they would've done so client for a potential sale), we end up doing one task less satisfactorily… sometimes to the detriment of life and health! If you're behind the wheel, focus on the road. If you're at work or school, list down the things you need to do that day. When you focus on a single activity, the focus itself distracts your mind from the anxiety.

6. <u>Don't be an all-or-nothing Annie</u> – Have you ever found yourself beginning a task (say clearing out the garage), only to give up soon as you start because it seems like an overwhelming undertaking? You're not alone. Rather than do everything on a one-time, big-time basis, chop your objective into chunks. Do a drawer here. Declutter a box over there. Need to gain/lose weight? Don't focus on the 15 stone you need to lose. Break your goal into a stone or even half a stone. When you accomplish small goals, completion gives you the confidence to repeat the process. Small goals count. And progress is progress no matter how small.

7. <u>Practice an attitude of gratitude</u> – There is always something to be thankful for. Some people would rather see the glass as half full. Go a step further and be thankful that you even have a glass! Make it a habit to express appreciation for the big and small things alike. Maintain a journal and jot down the things you are thankful for daily… hot running water, waking up, warm coffee, your baby's giggle, that pleasant walk through the office garden. Find that person who

makes a difference in your life and send a thank you note. Not a letter-writing person? Do something for someone whom you know can't pay you back. Buy breakfast for someone on the street. Volunteer for a soup kitchen. Teach someone to read. Finding the good in the daily grind will help you view the world differently.

A Fixed Mindset
V
A Growth Mindset.

People with a Fixed Mindset believe that their qualities are static, fixed, and cannot be changed. These individuals suppose that their talents, temperament, level of creativity and intelligence are set. They feel that there is no use working to develop and learn. Further, they tend to believe that talent, more than effort, leads to success.

On the other hand, people with a Growth Mindset believe that talent, intelligence, creativity, and learning can grow given experience, effort and time. They believe that they can become smarter with effort. They also believe that effort influences success, so they put in extra time, and thus achieve more.

FIXED MINDSET

Pros	Cons
Prevents short-term failure	Impedes your ability to develop new skills, learn, and grow
People who practice a Fixed Mindset as regards to their sexual orientation -- meaning they accept who they are and who they're meant to be, are better adjusted than those who feel that they should "change".	Low tolerance for failure and temporary setbacks.
	Easy successes and wrong praise discourages a "can-do" mentality
	Cultivates an "I should look smart" attitude

GROWTH MINDSET

Pros	Cons
Helps build confidence because you are constantly learning something new	If used incorrectly, can lead the person to believe that effort is all you need. May encourage ineffective

rather than ABILITY. So, if you're an adult learner, by all means... take that course. Learn that instrument. Attend that class. All you need to do is want it and put in the needed hours to learn the skill. If you're still in doubt, just think about John Basinger. He managed to memorize the 60,000-word poem, *Paradise Lost*, at the age of 67 --- only because he wanted to complement his physical exercise with mental callisthenics. It took him nine years of practice (and you certainly don't need to achieve the same feat), but if his mind was capable of such achievement, then so can yours.

4. My failures are learning experiences. Even flops teach me something.

I have not failed. I've just found 10,000 ways that won't work. – Thomas Edison

Nobody likes failure. But if you're reaching for an objective, a person with a Growth Mindset views failure as a great way to learn. Try again. If you should fail, fail better.

5. I look up to others who have been successful in their endeavours.

People with a Growth Mindset model their work after those who have been successful in similar work.

Those with a Fixed Mindset, on the other hand, see these people as a threat and someone to envy.

This shouldn't be the case. Role models are the proof you need to show that it is possible. Instead of feeding an envy mindset, take an interest in their work and the manner with which they were able to achieve their own goals. You'd be surprised to find that they probably failed more times than you can imagine.

6. *I value constructive criticism*

People don't take negative feedback kindly. Helpful criticism can feel like an insult, putting people on the defence. So, how can you use negative feedback to your advantage?

Show gratitude – Acknowledge that you are receiving points of improvement

Analyse the feedback given - Take a look at your work and be objective. You may find the feedback to be helpful.

Ask questions – Sometimes, it just boils down to understanding what you were told. Ask for specific points of improvement.

Create goals – With a specific point of improvement in mind, set goals to include the feedback given.

7. The results of my attempts don't define me.

It's easy to be defined by low tests scores, a rejected proposal, and numbers that describe a particular status (weight, salary grade, etc). However, if you focus on these alone, you're allowing yourself to fall under a Fixed Mindset.

You are not your numbers. Focus on daily, consistent, positive habits. These inevitably lead to growth and development.

8. Being uncomfortable is OK.

A ship in harbour is safe. But that's not what ships are built for" goes a well-loved adage.

New challenges (or anything new for that matter) can be overwhelming only because of the unknowns and the probability of failure. This Fixed Mindset can lead anyone to simply avoid challenges.

But nobody accomplished anything worthwhile whilst staying within a comfort zone. When you accept the reality of humps, bumps, and detours, you are more likely to take a risk and pursue a path – despite the barriers.

9. If this doesn't work for me, I will try a different approach.

A Growth Mindset is not just about working harder but working smarter. There are different styles of learning. Find out which one is yours and stick to it. Some learn faster via a visual (spatial) approach. Some learn by an aural (auditory-musical) approach. And yet others maximise learning through logical (mathematical), physical (kinaesthetic), or verbal (linguistic) means. For instance, if a new skill involves historical memory work, perhaps it would help to visit the place instead of just highlighting words on a textbook.

10. I believe in myself and my capabilities!

When you feel confident with your ability to learn and grow despite the obstacles you face, you are more likely to persevere. Confidence helps you bounce back quickly after a setback....and that alone is very empowering!

Talk Yourself into a Growth Mindset

A Fixed Mindset can be devious. When you get frustrated and make a mistake, what do you find yourself saying? How about when faced with an overwhelming challenge, what's your knee-jerk reaction statement?

Here are some Fixed Mindset thoughts and Mind Growth samples of what to say instead.

Instead of … (Fixed Mindset)
This is such a difficult math problem. I don't have the skillset for this.

Think …(Growth Mindset)
I can learn this. I just might need a mentor's help / to acquire the necessary skills.

Instead of:
I'm not good at this.

Think:
Am I missing something? If so, what am I missing?

Instead of:
My plan didn't go as intended.

Think:
What are my alternatives? What's plan B? C? D? Good thing the alphabet has so many letters left! Who can help me? Where can I get the help I need?

Instead of:
I give up!

Think:
What do I want? Maybe I should just try a different strategy? Maybe I should try rewording this project's objectives. I'll give it another go.

Instead of:
My head's a mess and I can't calm my thoughts!

Think:
I'm teaching my mind to focus.

Instead of:
Hey! I got this! I'm the best!

Think:
I'm on the right track!

Instead of:
This doesn't make sense / It doesn't make sense to do this?

Think:
What will make it "have" some sense? It doesn't make sense ... YET.

Morning routines

Whether you find yourself wearing the hat of a student, office worker, supervisor, parent, business owner, teacher, or whatever role you play daily, there will be days when you feel you want to start over.

"If only life had a reset button," you wonder. "Or even a Ctrl-Z command. Now, wouldn't that be awesome?"

Guess what… life hands you exactly that every day when you wake up.

Whatever a morning is to you (whether you get up when the sun rises or just when the moon does), here are some morning routines you may want to use to get you started on the right mindset!

1. Prepare the night before. Mornings are a frenzy. Lessen the stress by laying your clothing out, prepping your gym bag, and prepping yours (and the kids') lunches. Clear your mornings of errands that can agitate and stress. I found the best for me was a to-do list written the night before. American Express CEO Kenneth Chenault writes down three things he wants to accomplish the following day.

2. Get enough sleep. In his TEDx Talk, Williams College Biology Professor Dr. Matthew Carter emphasized how sleep can make or break our lives. Incorrect sleeping habits or sleep deprivation can wreak the same havoc as smoking and eating the worst types of food. Dr. Carter says that we should take our cue from our kids. Kids are the best sleepers because we give them a routine. We take the time to go to bed, bathe them, properly brush their teeth, read them a story, give them some water, turn of the lights… and they sleep very soundly once they do. Get a good night's

sleep - it's key to waking up great the next day! Five to eight hours of sleep is ideal.

3. When you get up, make your bed immediately. William H. McRaven, a retired United States Navy admiral, has been known for these famous words, *"If you want to change the world, start by making your bed."* The act of fixing your bed sets the tone for the day because you've accomplished your first important task. It may seem like an insignificant chore, but it isn't! Making your bed reinforces the idea that the little things matter in life. If you come home to a bed that is made, you set the tone for the next day – even if today didn't go as planned.

4. Avoid social media. It's easy to lose track of time with all the notifications. Psychologist Wilcox Stephen is of the belief that social media sites such as Facebook can only increase self-esteem in the very short term. But it can incite us to keep up with appearances and mask our true personas. It can also feed anxiety as we subconsciously seek acceptance and approval via these media.

5. Use the few minutes of quiet to be thankful. Today is a new leaf – no matter how dreadful the day before was. An attitude of gratitude goes a long way, and there is always something to be thankful for!

6. Is a cup of coffee your go-to in the morning? Why not try lukewarm water instead? People with a positive outlook tend to reach for water (sometimes with a splash of lemon) instead of coffee because the results are astounding. It helps them feel more alert (versus coffee) as it rehydrates your body and jump-starts their metabolism. Studies suggest we can dehydrate whilst asleep, and so water first thing in the morning is the best way to keep focused throughout the day.

7. Get your heart pumping at least three times a week. The wealthy and successful all prioritise health. Lift weights or head for the gym before anything else. Invest in an elliptical or treadmill. Prioritise and make time for physical exercise as you would an important appointment.

8. Meditate and set your intention – be in the moment. An excellent type of meditation anyone can do is simply being aware of what's happening in and around you. If you've got 5 minutes, you can meditate. Simply calm your mind. Don't think of tasks you need to accomplish just yet. Can't control your thoughts? Count your breath to focus. Haven't got 5 minutes? Be in the moment while going through your morning routine. Be conscious of the sound water makes or the whistling of the kettle. This is an excellent

technique to calm down. Tranquillity helps elicit positivity.

9. Check your plate. A balanced breakfast gives your body just the right fuel to tackle your day. Always include protein, healthy fat, and fibre. A quick breakfast would consist of scrambled eggs on whole-grain toast with slices of avocado. Throw in some yoghurt with nuts or berries. A good breakfast not only boosts energy, it helps your concentration and memory as well. When your mind is at its peak, productivity is off the roof.

10. Read. Whether it's on the commute to work or just after a lovely shower and cup of strong coffee, sit down and spend 20 minutes reading every morning. Before you know it, you're reading a book a month. That's half the amount read per year by Barack Obama!

11. Practice chunking. Neuroscientist Daniel Bor explains that chunking is our ability to access or "hack" the limits of our memory. It's a method that allows people to take small pieces of information and then combine them into meaning, easier-to-remember units. It's a great memory enhancer that you could do for a few minutes in the morning. Say, for instance, you want to remember items from a list. Form small groups that are similar (for instance, if trying to recall items from a

grocery list, divide into dairy items, fresh produce etc). Chunking is an everyday memory enhancer.

12. Make time for happiness. Spend time with friends and family. This need not be a huge gathering … even the simple act of eating breakfast together or making a quick call to a loved one can help boost your day.

Last but not least… smile. Smiling isn't just good for you; it positively affects others as well! A study by The British Dental Health Association showed that smiling can affect our mood dramatically. Feeling down? Forcing a smile can significantly improve your mood. It helps reduce the symptoms of anxiety such as digestion problems and elevated blood pressure. Also, smiling activates the neurotransmitters associated with pleasure – dopamine, serotonin, and endorphins. Your smile is a natural pain reliever and instant mood lifter! So, make the conscious decision every morning to be happy, grateful and respectful to others. Often those that don't smile need it the most.

The benefits of smiling don't end there. In a study conducted by the Face Research Laboratory (the University of Aberdeen in Scotland), men and women were more enticed by photos or images depicting people who smiled and made eye contact. They theorise that smiling makes you look more confident, sincere, attractive, and relaxed. And of course, when someone smiles at you, your immediate reaction is to smile back. Win-win.

Mindsets of Successful people – 7 Hacks:

When we see successful people thriving in their lives and endeavours (be it a business, sport, or project), we often wonder what is it that makes them achieve more. Successful people have many positive traits and habits. A common denominator for them is a positive outlook and a Growth Mindset.

Here's a peek into how they think …

1. They know and accept themselves

Bill Gates and J.K. Rowling are introverts. But that didn't stop them from excelling in their fields. They know their strengths and accept their weaknesses. If they don't possess a skill set necessary to accomplish a goal, they either find someone who does or create ways and means to achieve it.

2. They set goals that are in line with their values, interests, skills, strengths, and purpose

Steve Jobs, Martin Luther King Jr, Nelson Mandela all lived their lives based on what they valued and what they were good at. Some had to pay a high price for pursuing their goals, but we doubt that any of them would have taken the easier route.

3. They drop the fixed mindset

When they feel that their game isn't tops, they don't just sit and accept the status quo. They take steps to make progress. A Fixed Mindset dictates that things won't change no matter the effort. A Growth Mindset, on the other hand, says that you CAN initiate change through effort, hard work, accepting feedback, and implementing strategies. To them, it all boils down to empowering beliefs. Believe you can, and you will.

4. They're willing to fail

You might be surprised to hear that the most successful people on the planet aren't the ones who never failed. They're the ones who have failed the most! The fear of failure can be paralysing – so much so that some entrepreneurs fail because they fear to start a new endeavour in the first place. *"Pain is inevitable. Suffering is optional."*, says the Dalai Lama. Successful people struggle (they struggle a lot!), but they don't think of it as suffering because they know that they are on track to pursuing a goal. Successful people agree that tough times are inevitable.

5. They seek the best, not perfection

The pursuit of perfection is strongly connected to stress, anxiety, and burnout. Successful people have lofty goals, but they are also realistic. They know that progress is progress ... and they never stop pursuing it.

6. They take risks

Former Yahoo! CEO Marissa Meyer says that she would always do something she was "a little ready NOT to do." It was how she grew. That moment of not being sure that she could push her through those difficult moments was when she would have a breakthrough. Truly, growth and comfort don't co-exist, says Ginni Rometty, CEO IBM. These women know that success comes to those who go out on a limb.

7. They always invest in themselves

Books, education, courses, family, business relations ... successful people enrich themselves through continuous improvement, learning, and self-education. Warren Buffet is a huge advocate for learning. To him, the most important investment one can make is in oneself. Warren Buffet began with $100 and turned it into $30 billion – which goes to show that it isn't how much money you have, but the knowledge you have.

Bonus tip: is to ask for help, even if you don't think you need it.

How often have you said, "I can figure this out; I want to do it myself?" What you really mean is "I don't want to accept help, because that means you are smarter than me. Because I have no self-esteem, I need to act like I know what to do all the time." Accepting help is okay – it doesn't mean you have to take all of the advice, but at least listen to others to see if what they say is helpful. Whoever can support you or show you the way doesn't matter. The end result is the only thing that matters.

A good reaction is, "If you can teach me how to do something easier, better or quicker, then I would like to learn from you." It's not because you are dumb when you can't figure out how to get what you want. It's because you are not trained to see beyond your present consciousness level. There is a tendency in the industry to lock up conventional approaches. "This is how we always have done it." We blind ourselves to the way it could be when we use that kind of thought and hang on to the way it was.

For further resources, courses and coaching please visit www.mindsetmastership.com

Chapter 4: To Gain Achievements, Success is Mandatory

"There are two types of people who will tell you that you cannot make a difference in this world: those who are afraid to try and those who are afraid you will succeed." -Ray Goforth

Introduction

There is no description of failure. Success can't be described either. Some people feel they are successful with luxury cars and wealth, while others flourish with their loved ones. You need to have your own definition of success. If you already have skills and a talent, harness that energy, and learn to develop it.

4.1. Techniques of Success

Commitment is the first necessity; commitments have to be made in life to achieve anything. Commitment and positive power clarify your goals. More importantly, it motivates you to succeed. You need to know how important it to show full commitment to your goals. How far you can go to reach your goals must be discovered.

Don't think about the outcomes; concentrate on learning. Insecurity about the outcomes makes it difficult for you to achieve your goals. Your personal life is also being obstructed. Your strengths are the key to success.

Analyse how you do a job and identify where changes are needed. Through discovery and innovation, don't hesitate to make adjustments. You are inspired to achieve your goals. If you are a student, you may feel unmotivated because your results may be poor, or you feel your job prospects are limited. Don't fret - seek assistance. You can find help online these days. It reduces pressure and lets you focus on learning more.

You should believe in the power of positivity and believe your journey is enjoyable. You have to take in all your life experiences. You will lose perspective if you begin to worry too much about the problems you encounter on the journey. It will stop you from advancing, and you may not succeed.

You get two kinds of thoughts in your mind – positive or negative. These two thoughts affect your emotions and perceptions. You have the option to choose one of these two. Positive thoughts are the better choice. They will allow you to work effectively and will also keep your morale up.

In life, imagination is key to feeling happy and generating energy. At times, using the power of creative thoughts can often be the key to victory. You have good feelings and think it's all going to happen.

But if you face life's difficulties, you reduce positive energy and then imagination becomes charged with negative thoughts.

Therefore, wash the negativity away with optimistic thinking any time you imagine something unwanted. Try to understand how you will feel after your goals have been achieved. Imagine how thrilling your successful journey will be. The power of positivity and creativity will help you keep your dreams alive.

There are two types of people. The first type sits back and waits for openings, and the second type pushes themselves, takes responsibility and does things.

Don't hate the obstacles; you want to test yourself. The challenges are mostly successful. So, if the obstacles you face are the key to success, what are you waiting for? What do you expect? Figure out what frightens you on your way to your goals and be ready to face these challenges and succeed.

Avoid distractions around you. It may be difficult to study if your place of study is continuously noisy. If you receive regular Facebook or other social media updates, you may not concentrate on your work. It is, therefore, a must for you to avoid such distractions when carrying out any mission. Focus on the things that are most essential. This helps you to do your work successfully.

It's good to take the advice of others and then do things independently. Relying on others for everything is not ideal. Therefore, you should believe in constructive power and try working on all ventures independently. You should also accept some of your friends' support or advice if they have time.

Plan and check your progress periodically. If you don't know the way, you can't reach your target. Preparing the way to success allows you to explore. This lets you know what you're going to do and how you are going to do it. This is your achievement in preparation.

In addition, you will periodically check each job. During your analysis, you will take a critical approach. Your vulnerable points must be identified. It's also a must to find ways to strengthen your weaknesses.

4.2. How to Make Your Day Productive

Now you know that positivity is the key to success and the best approach. Another important thing is to make your day productive. Therefore, let's see some tips that can help you. Beginning in the morning, get up early, have a drink and a healthy breakfast, and go for a walk. This is how many successful people start their day. Next, when you go to work; identify the main tasks that you have to complete. The tasks must be prioritized and attempted in the first part of the day.

The first half of the day is fresh for tackling challenging tasks. However, some people do more than one job at a time or multitask; an ability few people have. Nevertheless, research has shown that attempting multiple tasks affect the quality of work. Therefore, one job at a time is encouraged. That is another major factor for success.

Many people spend hours working on their jobs. Learn to manage your time. The effect of overworking is burnout or exhaustion. Some people take a number of breaks when carrying out a job that they cannot manage. You must balance work with breaks, and work with determination and confidence in the power of positivity. But don't think of taking long breaks - the duration of the breaks must be managed.

Don't forget to test yourself and check your own performance throughout the day. No matter the success of your day, self-assessment is important. Any mistakes you made throughout a mission must be identified. You should know where you have done wrong.

A positive attitude is always related to success. Positivity lets you discover immense possibilities and keeps you both confident and motivated. It is, therefore, easy to succeed if you believe in positive power. You can build a positive attitude more quickly than you can imagine. Positive thoughts do not allow your mind to have any doubts.

You will see amazing changes all around you when you learn how to think positively. In reality, the brain begins to pump in free-flowing, feel-good hormones called endorphins, making you feel lighter and more relaxed. You will also notice a huge increase in confidence and will feel more capable than ever before. Your comfort zone of taking up new tasks and challenges will be high.

You will easily unlock your brakes and witness development as you never dreamed by reducing your self-restraining beliefs. Ultimately, through the use of the power of positive thinking, you will change your entire life.

4.3. The Initiation of Success

Since the beginning of time, all great teachers have aimed to make us aware that we continue building our own reality. Most importantly, we are responsible for everything in our lives, which means the good, the bad and the ugly.

We still look outside of ourselves for the answer if we assume that we are being harmed. We must first look within ourselves to get accurate answers to our issues so that we can see people and events in a new way. The outside world is a mirror of our inner world in many ways. You've got to know that. Who did not give this question any consideration? How many troubled people do you know? Until we look beyond ourselves to find the answer, no commitment, no desire, no encouragement or motivation can fix our problems.

Chapter 5: Factors Governing Mindset

"The mind is just like a muscle - the more you exercise it, the stronger it gets and the more it can expand."-
Idowu Koyenikan

5.1. Law of Attraction

Like all natural laws, the law of attraction functions with statistical precision. It's neutral and impersonal, so it works if you want it to. It doesn't have anything to do with your temperament, religious beliefs, morals or your wealth status.

The Law of Attraction is as accurate as the Law of Gravity - an irrefutable law. No one understood gravity before the law of gravity was known, and yet it still influenced everyone. The Law of Attraction is similar. Many people don't understand the mechanics, but everyone knows it works. Just like you don't need to understand how the Law of Gravity works in order to stop you from floating into space, you don't need to understand the mechanics of how the Law of Attraction functions in your life.

You may not have known this, but you are drawn to everything you encounter in your life. Maybe that's not good news if your life hasn't been going as you want. And since most of us are unhappy with what we have produced in our lives, we've become masters of attracting an influx of negative circumstances.

You need to become aware of the unconscious patterns of thought that control our lives, as we attract what we envision. The primary role of the subconscious mind is to be directed by the conscious mind. This is achieved by "proving" that anything the conscious mind thinks is real. So, if you believe that you can't do something or can't have what you want, the subconscious creates circumstances to find proof that you are 'right.'

The world around you is not altered by your subconscious. It only filters the data you provide to support the image you have in mind. When, for instance, you think business is bad, or your company has no new opportunities, your subconscious can neglect potential ways of improving your business. It only suggests problems that affirm your belief that things are bad, or that new opportunities do not exist. You will bring nothing more to yourself than things which are compatible with your deepest inner convictions. You will feel powerless to change your life for the better if you do not understand that you build your reality with your thoughts. Instead, you will believe that you are a victim of other people, situations and circumstances.

If you consider yourself to be powerless, you must look for something or someone outside of yourself to fulfil your needs. Through clear thinking, you will realise that you can give yourself what you want, and you can create everything that you want.

5.2. Have Faith in your Creative Power

You must trust the Power within you to build what you want. Now, when you're told to trust the Power inside yourself, you might say, "But, see the poverty. See the illnesses, the conflict and the violence in the world. If this "Power" existed, why would any of these things happen?"

We can use this power to create everything in our lives that we want. Everything comes from our thoughts. In other words, it's done to you as you think, not as you want. Now, what would you do if you wanted more power? You would generate less resistance to handle the additional power flow.

You and I are imaginative people, and we are always able to build more. We create, knowingly or unconsciously all the time. By realising who we are, we can start moving our creation from the unconscious to the conscious through the cycle of expanding the energy inside.

5.3. Your Unlimited Power

Controlling your thoughts is in your power. A distracted mind can lead you to sickness, misery, scarcity and restriction instead of towards wealth, health and achievement. We are creating from our unconscious if we do not make our lives the way we want them to be. But as life is consciousness, the most important task that we have is to achieve the highest knowledge. We can do it, even if our pride is challenged by looking at the situation of our lives and questioning our beliefs.

Chapter 6: Know the Truth about Yourself

"If you tell the truth, you don't have to remember anything." - Mark Twain

You must have a basic understanding of who you are if you want to have control over your life. The key to a successful life is creating your own self-image. This image is compatible with your attitude, thoughts, behaviours and even your skills. Be the type of person you claim to be. False identities can harden your self-image. Either you are happy and successful with yourself, or you oppress your life.

The circumstances that shaped your self-image may have been a misunderstanding or blown out of proportion, but they are real for you. Once you know why you feel a certain way, your feelings are valid. You can believe something is true even if it's not true.

You have to know who you are as a person, and what you are not. Who we are could be morally perfect, but what we do is not always ideal. If we don't consider ourselves spiritually perfect, our actions will be less than perfect.

6.1. Ego

Your ego fools you and convinces you of what is untrue. It wants you to look down upon yourself. It makes you identify with all that you are not. It would like you to criticise, denounce and blame yourself for not meeting your goals and other expectations. You must know you are being fooled by your ego. It doesn't usually speak the truth.

Note, one of the most important steps to changing your life is to know that you are spiritually complete and good no matter what you want to be or have. To neutralise your ego, you must love yourself unconditionally.

You have to realise that life is about mindfulness. What you believe to be reality is your own truth. When your habits of thought say, "I cannot have this or that, I don't deserve it, I am a bad person," and so forth, you keep creating circumstances that limit your opportunities.

The bottom line is this: you must accept that you are worthy and deserving of yourself.
The solution is for you to develop unconditional love. This is the only way you can be at a safer place.

6.2. You Create Yourself

You have built yourself whether or not you know it. You borrowed, imitated or made yourself all the traits of character, mannerisms, ways of speaking, facial expressions, gestures and even ways of thinking and believing. You may have been influenced by your mother, a favourite teacher, a relative, or a character in a book or film. Perhaps you borrowed a trait that you don't like. For example, perhaps you imitate traits from a person who made you feel nervous or scared. Imitating that person might help you feel less fearful and intimidated.

6.3. Never Belittle Yourself

It is essential to take a look at your personality. Perhaps if you are an imitator, you have difficulty identifying yourself. Giving up on this is not unusual. It might help to understand that no one can build themselves from scratch.

Even if you may have built your personality by imitation, you are not a fraud. Nobody else has ever had the exact same mix of traits as you. Consider this: there are only twelve musical notes, and yet several hundred thousand unique and beautiful combinations are made. Everything depends on how these combinations are organised. Imitating parts of a personality doesn't make you any less special than someone else. The beautiful thing about this is that you can change it anytime because YOU put it together from scratch. You are never trapped. You are never stuck. It's okay if you find you're not the person you thought you were. Consider it the start of something new.

6.4. Self-Acceptance is Freedom

The ego can cause you to feel that you are incompetent, inadequate, dangerous, dumb, poor, bad and unworthy. This can reduce your self-confidence and produce a poor self-image. Unless you make a conscious decision to change your thinking patterns, you will continue to have poor self-esteem and poor self-image. You must embrace yourself to love yourself. You can only start loving others when you respect yourself.

Some people say that you ought to forget about yourself and just love others. Well, that's not how it works. The fact is, you have to recognise yourself with all your errors — all your so-called sins, every time you looked like a follower, and every time you did wrong.

The way you see yourself influences your actions and determines your performance. No matter how hard you try, someone will think you are doing something wrong. Remember this: in someone's eyes, you will always be a failure. You can't win everybody over. You just can't please everyone, so you must learn to please yourself and like who you are. It is worth remembering that who you are is perfect in spirit, but what you do is not always perfect. Just know that you cannot fail as a person in your life. That's not how you are built.

Whether you blame yourself or others for the things you did or did not do, you are in pain. Suffering is a way to get down to it and allow yourself to be upset. Maybe you did not live up to a dream that you had for yourself. Maybe you didn't live up to someone else's expectations. Self-hatred is one of the main causes of self-destructive behaviour. Many of us judge ourselves by what we have or don't have, and what we have accomplished or not accomplished.

If we do not live up to the standards of our families, bosses, or peers, we might decide that we are just no good. This is referred to as self-judgment. You might judge yourself as unworthy. As soon as you're criticised for something you've done or something you haven't figured out, you feel bad. Moreover, this kind of criticism sculpts the little self-esteem you have. It's never healthy; it's damaging. Every person has moments they regret, but they must stop regretting and move on at some point.

6.5. How you Treat Yourself Forms the Basis of your Mindset

Questions to ask yourself:

-Do you like yourself?
-Do you have confidence in yourself?
-Do you deliver on your promises?
-Do you think you're a good person?
-Would you create an act to cover up who you are?
-Would you keep someone like you as a friend?

Looking at how we deal with ourselves is very important. Often, I hear people say, "I want to explore my inner-self, but I am afraid of what I will find out about myself. I am afraid of strange discoveries which I may find along the way." We're our own worst enemy most of the time.

Chapter 7: Self-Discovery

*"Knowing yourself is the beginning
of all wisdom."* - Aristotle

Start your self-discovery journey right away. Nothing but good can come out of it. Understanding your fear helps to heal the fear. Don't worry if you're better or worse than other people. Try to know yourself, instead, as the type of person you are and the person you want to become.

You don't condemn a semi-finished house while it is still under construction - you just know that you need to do more work. Take this approach to yourself. Regardless of your current condition, just realise that you need more construction. Be gentle with yourself but be adamant about the required work.

Self-worth: You will never be able to love yourself if you feel your value comes from what others think.

A self-aware person understands his personality, and he knows all about those who are of the same sort. Know who you are, and you will know how many others are like you.

Do not be afraid to reveal yourself, even if what you are revealing seems like a disadvantage. Power begins when you acknowledge your weaknesses. It's always good that you know your weaknesses, no matter how difficult or shocking they may be. Keep this in mind, especially in times when you know you must give up on something but feel unable to do so. Having the courage to recognise your weaknesses helps you change yourself.

If you learn the truth about yourself and live your life as you want, many people will not approve because they are unable to go the same way as you. Should you deny your own wealth because other people are poor? Should you reject feeling well because there are millions of sick people? Look carefully into what you deny yourself and never think of yourself as "fake" because of your wishes.

We are bound to make mistakes on our path to self-discovery. You are not those so-called mistakes, flaws or sins. Make sure you differentiate who you are from what you have and do. You know that what happens in life is fleeting and will always change. You have to realise that your Higher Self is unchanging. When you identify with your temporary nature, you accept that you are what you have, and you are what you do. It may be the biggest mistake you make in your life.

As you stand on the seaside and look at boats sailing around, there is no problem as long as you just stand and watch them go through. You will only experience pain and suffering if you interact with the vessels. You might grieve when it passes by your sight if you say, "That's MY ship." You might live in fear of someone else being its captain by thinking, "I must command that ship." Likewise, if we take on passing issues as our own, we may feel responsible for errors and faults just by merely observing them.

When you begin to question your life and examine it honestly, you come to the point where you realise that the only source of authority is you. Though you might be waiting for others to tell you what you need to do, you alone know what to do. Maybe you don't want to be responsible for your own life, or you'd rather other people make decisions for you. But understand this truth: So long as you allow other people to be responsible for your future, they govern your destiny.

7.1. Change your World

It is easy to say that others are to blame for our problems, but this way of thinking binds us further because we limit our independence. We are to blame.

Again, to straighten your thinking means to separate what you have from who you are. Separate the "doer" from the "deed." In our current culture, the trick is to live but to disallow the world to live in us.

Let me ask you before I go any further: "Why do you want your world to change?" We need to improve our perspectives.

When you return to the fundamental principle of life, you realise that in the universe, nothing happens that you cannot accept deep within your consciousness. Some things have been done to you, as you believe, and these convictions are sometimes very strong. Everything takes place within our minds, even though we may not be aware of it, is in profound harmony with our experiences without it. I know it is difficult to embrace the rule because you don't want things in your life.

The reality is, however, that you are meeting a deep inner desire. Imagine an unhappy person sitting in his house, saying, "I want to change my life." Then he's as sad as he was before. He redecorates many times, but to himself, he still has no sense of change.

Do you know people who believe their happiness will improve by altering their outer landscape? Where did that error come from? How can they correct themselves?

You can discover what is happening if you are fully honest with yourself and take a good look at what is happening in your life. This process of self-evaluation is an excellent way to find yourself if you no longer know what to do.

The truth is, you are not what you have, and you are not what you do. Your spiritual completion, completeness and perfection are in direct proportion to your ability to accept this reality about yourself.

7.2. Identify your Goals

"Setup the mind for the best," this will be discussed in depth later. But, for now, you only need to realise that looking at a photo isn't like watching a film. If the picture cannot be identified, you won't remember it because the image is not registered in the subconscious level.

In your image, you will "shadow" yourself. The final result is intentional reinforcement or self-talk, paired with visualisation. If we keep visualising it again and again, our subconscious will agree that it's real for us very soon.

In the beginning, there is tension between where you are or what you have and what you implicitly embrace. Nevertheless, one of the main functions of the unconscious is to solve conflicts between what we think about and what we live by. And because our subconscious is creative, what we think of and visualise begins to be created.

First of all, you need to change your image. Real growth and improvement start from within. Your comfort zone will naturally grow, and you will act accordingly to your new truth or religion.

How do you know what your self-image is? Accept your actions, attitudes and results. Also, ask yourself, "What do I expect of myself? Where do I feel out of place?" You will unconsciously do things to let yourself be lost if you see yourself as poor. What do you think you say to yourself when you lose? "I've never got money." This reinforces your image, which triggers your self-talk again, which enhances the picture, and thus continues. "I'm like that," "I'm still lost," "I never have cash."

People feel oppressed without money, but what they don't understand is that they live a self-fulfilling prophecy. This is why wealthy people get wealthier and the poor stay poor. It doesn't have anything to do with money.

Those with winning self-images do winning things. They don't accept losing as their destiny if they lose occasionally. You know it's not natural for you to lose. You deny it by saying, "That wasn't like me" or "This doesn't happen to me."

7.3. Your Attitude Affects your Success

Understanding the difference between success and failure is crucial. Attitudes are prevailing convictions. The assessment of an attitude is always objective. Once you have set a goal, an attitude can either help you achieve it or prevent you from reaching your target.

People are often looking for problems or ways to avoid problems because of the attitudes they created. Most of these attitudes were unintentionally created.

If you have an attitude that causes you to avoid situations, you can make a conscious decision to change. All you have to do is make a new statement, visualise the end result, and re-imagine yourself as a person with the attitude you desire. You can see yourself looking for a particular action in daily life, or in some cases avoid, if you choose.

You shall either remain where you are or persuade yourself that it is in your best interest to change with deliberate intention. If you choose to change, you must imagine your new belief. Constructive self-talk and imagination help you evolve without anxiety, pressure and negative feedback in a controlled way.

People have a certain self-image for different aspects of their lives. My subconscious must ensure that I always do what is real. My self-image influences my success in how I behave or act.

We want to focus on our self-image rather than relying on our actions. How are we doing? We begin to regulate our self-talk so that when our behaviour becomes different than how we want it to be, we will say to ourselves, "That is not how I am. That's not like me." Our images are controlled by direct self-talk.

We can imagine a new behaviour, even if it is the opposite of our attitude or actions right now. Make sure the behaviour is tested to achieve the desired end result. When the picture you imagine changes, the output will change as well.

In relation to the goal, our subconscious imaginative process knows precisely where we are in time and place. This stimulates creative energy and drives people to look at material things, new books, seminars or anything else to create our images. But the first picture has to come. Without an image, we can't begin.

This unconscious imaginative process gives you a strategy to use your creative skills. It is essential to control what you are picturing. It needs to be established clearly and explicitly. What is it? How is it? You can't have it if you can't describe it.

7.4. Never Force Change – That is failure

"I must lose weight" "I must work harder." That very pressure is unconsciously working against the end results you seek. The greatest pit that we fall into is forcing change, like trying to control ourselves and telling ourselves, "I must do this."

If you think you have to do something, it's your job to say, "No, you don't have to do anything." And with clever diversion, delay, or any way you can, you find a way to stop it. If you think, 'I must,' then you can say, 'But I would rather do something else.' The harder you try to do something, the more you work against your artistic subconscious.

I have strength in me that most people have given up, because I know I can make a difference, because it's my idea to be like that. I should stop saying "I have to," and say "I can." I will be as my imagination tells me, I can and will step constructively towards that end result with exciting magnetic energy and drive. I know that I am a self-made individual, that both succeeds and fails, and that this success or failure is my power. You become a powerful person when you rely on commitments to yourself and others. You are just as strong as your word.

When you give your word to other people that you will be somewhere at a certain time, you have to be able to follow through, because every time you don't hold your word, you lose control. You need to be able to depend on yourself to do what you say you will do.

Keep your mind open about what you want and don't want to do. Do not spend time thinking about what you are trying to avoid. Go towards what you want rather than trying to get away from what you don't want. Every moment is a new start. High-performing successful people look at what they want and work toward the final result. So, what do you want? That's what you need to know. Does it make you happy? Why are you going to work? Why should you go to school? Why do you get involved? For yourself, what do YOU want?

When you do what you like to do – purposefully – you will draw in people and situations that are needed to help you serve your mission. Understand, you're drawn to what you believe and visualise. Start by understanding where you want to go and start talking about it with yourself.

Chapter 8: Seeing is Believing

"Faith is to believe what you do not see; the reward of this faith is to see what you believe." - Saint Augustine

There is a general belief that "If I see it, it is true." We've also learned that people do not always adhere to the facts, but to their understanding of the truth.

8.1. Success Suffers a Setback due to Perception of Reality

People who have to see things before they can believe in them, or who need specific advice before they take a risk, probably find growing and changing to be difficult. They spend most of their lives waiting for something instead of doing it.

Our perception of reality is limited in the use of our imagination. We have to take a good look to see if our perception of reality is perhaps skewed or distorted in order to change it.

Even though we are all in the same universe, we interpret what we see differently.

All our decisions and actions are based on our awareness at any given moment. To be all that we can potentially be, our awareness or our perception of reality must constantly be changed and expanded.

A misperception of the majority of people is that "seeing is believing." But the fact is, just because we can't see something, doesn't mean it isn't there. The first thing that you have to ask yourself is, what is important or valuable to me? What am I looking for, and what are the results I want? You can't achieve goals until you understand exactly what you want. By knowing exactly what you want - what kind of home, job, vehicle, income, or, relationships; you increase your knowledge of useful resources and data that will help you achieve your target.

Naturally, our brain filters out knowledge which is of no interest to us or threatens our safety. The knowledge will start to flow through once we decide what we want. Remember, it doesn't mean it doesn't exist because we can't see it. It only means that we block information that we currently don't care about.

This is a necessary shielding mechanism that prevents us from becoming crazy. This mechanism can, however, restrict our opportunities if left unchecked.

A great deal of information is available at any given time to help you build what you want. Nonetheless, most people try to solve problems without deciding precisely what they want to achieve.

8.2. Focusing on the End Result

What do you need to know to get the end result you want? Here's an example of focusing on the end result: suppose you are interested in a specific car. Your mind is made up; you plan to buy no other car. Then everywhere you look, you see this car. Why does this happen? It's because your mind is now set on this particular brand.

This method can be used to find the customers, jobs, businesses or individuals you want to engage with. As soon as you know who or what you are looking for, you will find them/it. If you don't know what you are searching for, you won't find it.

8.3. Think Outside your Limitations

We don't see possibilities because we restrict the way we think. We have to be prepared to think outside our limits. If we encounter opposing thoughts, views or behaviours at the same time, we sometimes feel emotionally uncomfortable. Once anxiety comes in, we rationalise very quickly why we should stop, give up, or why we can't do something. Generally, a change in attitude is necessary to reduce the anxiety caused by the change.

Rationalisation is the most common way of alleviating disputes. Rationalisation is what people use when they try to explain why they do what they do. To avoid looking foolish, a person gathers information that supports their opinion or their behaviour. For example, there is a tendency to only see the good features of a person and ignore any of the negative characteristics.

Ironically, we block knowledge that may be useful for rational decisions, and ultimately blind ourselves from other alternatives. We feel the need to try and prove that we are correct. You can use your subconscious to help you find ideas and responses, but you use the same subconscious to justify why it cannot be achieved. You always have the choice, and you always have the option.

8.4. What We Think, We Attract

Sometimes you don't feel like doing or getting what you really want. The bigger your self-worth, the greater your interest, the more opportunities and the more risks you will take. An honest self-worth person says, "I can do everything I want to do."

Chapter 9: Create your Own Story

"Most of us have only one story to tell. I don't mean that only one thing happens to us in our lives: there are countless events, which we turn into countless stories. But there's only one that matters, only one finally worth telling." - Julian Barnes

Every human being has an inherent desire to achieve their potential. Three principal convictions in life keep us from being happy and satisfied: The first is: what I have is not better than what others have. The grass is always greener on the other side. The second belief is that it is easier to have more: more would be better regardless of how much I have. The third conviction is: I'll be happy if I get what I want. Is that really true?

9.1. Is your life about Problems or Solutions?

The success ethic described simply says, "When you get what you want, you're going to be happy." It's based on the theory that one day we'll be happy if we work harder and solve every problem in our lives.

All the problems you have to solve and how hard you have to work are the first things many of us think about when we get up in the morning. We were trained to think about what is not, what should be, what shouldn't be, and how we should fix or change a situation. But if you look honestly into your life, solving problems, working hard, and having all of the things you want will not radically change the quality of your life. Indeed, focusing on these areas has probably diminished the fun and excitement of living your best life.

Assume your life will be changed by a new job. You've got a new job, and quite quickly it's the same old thing; you're dealing with taking responsibility, meeting deadlines and working with others who are not so well-informed. You will then realise that this new job didn't make a big difference in how you feel, so something else needs to be found to satisfy you.

Perhaps you think your life will improve with a new mate, a new home, a baby, or more money. You might get those things eventually, but still aren't happy.

The explanation is clear. Nothing else will ever make us happy because happiness is an internal experience. It begins by being.

Our intentions are vibrations setting the universe in motion

Did you ever wonder why New Year resolutions do not work? What happens is that we are always saying things like "I will no longer eat candy," "I will stop screaming at the boys," "I will stop eating too much." But remember that New Year resolutions weren't about what you wanted. It's a kind of negative self-talk about what you don't want, rather than a picture of what you do want.

Setting objectives is an important factor that will determine your success or failure. Have you ever been on a business trip without at least knowing where you were going?

Have you ever played tennis without knowing where the courtyard was?

Would you leave to go shopping without having any idea of how to get there?

Have you ever been on holiday without realising where you were going?

"I want to be spontaneous. I want to be free to change my mind." Well, sometimes we falsely believe that freedom means avoiding commitment. Ultimately, our capacity to make decisions and commitments is true freedom. Our question is "What do I really want?" Start from a place where you know what you want on some level. You will decide at some point.

Keep this in mind - if you don't know what you want, then someone else is going to choose for you. It won't end up being what you really want because it was someone else's decision.

Chapter 10: Success, Mindset and Law of Attraction

"Try not to become a man of success. Rather become a man of value." - Albert Einstein

---

"The true measure of success is how many times you can bounce back from failure." - Stephen Richards

---

Your way of thinking and spirituality influences your life, from how you think and feel about what you are doing and how you respond to the world around you.

Here are eight powerful ways to improve your thoughts:

- Adjust your negative self-talk to a self-empowering talk. It sounds cliché, but it works to say, "I can do it," or "I got this." The mind will then open up new ways of thinking to help achieve your goal.

- Adjust your language: To promote a positive attitude, avoid phrases such as "I'm always like that," or "I always do that." Make it a habit, instead of moaning about your problems, to talk about things that go well in your life.

- Find out what mindset you need to achieve a goal and ask, "What thinking do I need to accomplish that goal?" and "what is the thought of people who succeeded in this?"

- Identify and conquer your personal limiting beliefs that keep you from achieving your full potential of mind.

- To grasp and change your ideas, read the books about the workings of the mind and brain. Learn through online courses, activities and training from experts in learning. Here are some of my favourite mental resources: Carol Dweck's insight into the growth mentality, everything from Gabrielle Bernstein.

- You want to boost your money & success? Surround yourself with people who display positive attitudes. Start a social circle with people who are doing what you want to be doing. When you see what is effective for other people, it is easier to adjust to a new way of thinking.

- Create new ways to help change your thinking - incorporate effective ways of thinking that can change your mind and strengthen your thought.

Actively search for opportunities that can help you grow and learn.

- Step out of your comfort zone: You have no choice but to stand up for this occasion and refine your ideas. When you encounter circumstances that threaten you. It's survival.

10.1. Manifesting Success Using the Law of Attraction

Since "The Secret" became popular, the Law of Attraction has become a big phrase. I strongly believe in the power of attraction. Our thoughts generate a flow of energy, and this energy is identical to our thoughts. So, if you concentrate on how much your day sucks, guess what? Crappier experiences will draw you in.

You'll have a much more positive experience and pull positive things into your life if you're in a headspace reflecting on everything that you're thankful for during your day.

How do you carry this willing abundance into your life? Take the following steps:

- Be very specific about what you want to put into your life. If you want a new job, make a list of everything you need to be happy with the job.

- Write your goals down. Research has revealed that you can accomplish your goals 42 per cent more when they are written down. Most specifically, focus on how you will understand all of these things.

- Imagine that you already have what you want. Schedule time to sit every day and envision your ideal feelings. Consider this like your daily meditation, where you can already see yourself with what you want. Maybe imagine yourself in a new office, running your own business, or driving that new car. The more you envision, the more you will truly believe it's on your way.

- Clear any mental blocks. You can tell the world all day long what you want, but if you think you are not worthy or good enough to receive what you envision, you're going to remain wherever you are.

- Have patience. Trying to quickly manipulate and force things to happen is just a way to mess up what the universe tries to do. Make sure you take steps every day to get your goals forward but know that nothing is in a hurry.

10.2. Achieve your Financial Desires

I am sure you have heard the saying that "the rich get richer and the poor get poorer." Those who are wealthy always talk about money. Those who experience poverty constantly think of misery, so it becomes a promise of self-fulfilment. The economy, recession, unemployment, interest rates or jobs have nothing to do with our success. It's because rather than focusing on what we want, we're focused on what we don't want.

The reality is that we are the makers of our own financial state. We have either sufficient or insufficient responsibilities. We must recognise this obligation before a change can be made. We reflect our negative thoughts if we feel financially trapped.

Our culture is dominated by thoughts about money and they can be pleasant or disturbing. Money cannot make you happy, but many things that make you unhappy can be done away with. Cash, whether you like it or not, will always be an important part of your life. Wealth decides the quality of your life in most situations because money gives you independence. You can either bear the agony of financial problems or use your power to solve these problems as a Deliberate Creator.

All too many people just survive - they live from paycheck to paycheck. The biggest cause of stress for the majority of adults is money problems. Because money problems can harm our wellbeing, disrupt our personal relationships, our jobs and our happiness, it should be at the top of our list to build financial stability and wealth.

We must clear up our old ideas, values and principles that prohibit us from living with wealth. This can include removing our incorrect convictions; money is tight, jobs are scarce, the economic situation isn't good for businesses, it's hard to become wealthy, or that maybe we don't deserve to be rich. Instead of the illusions we have, we need to fill our consciousness with the facts. We will ultimately affirm our own reality.

We can change our reality using statements like:

- I want to learn how to be rich.
- I have decided to gain riches.
- The sales are greater than the outflow, I get to pick.
- I allow myself to enjoy the money.
- I agree to alleviate my reluctance to be rich.
- I accept the money has just come into my life.
- I'm rich in dollars.

10.3. Create Wealth with Imagination

We always create from our imagination, but we don't understand how. We use the past to create the future and the present. Use your imagination and visualisations to create how you would like to build your life. Don't imagine it the way it was. If you do, the limitations of your past will form your future.

We must also contribute and share what we have with others. Our knowledge of our prosperity is growing each time we consider the resources we think we already have. When we increase our knowledge of our resources, our lives become more plentiful.

10.4. Be grateful – that's Being Positive

Recognise and be grateful for what you already have. Love what you have at the moment, no matter how little it seems when compared to what other people have. Instead of complaining, just appreciate what you have now. The old saying goes, "I cried because I didn't have a pair of shoes until I met a man with no feet."

Build an "attitude of thankfulness" for anything you have now and see how it will grow and grow. Buy and retain the 'Universal Bank ' definition. Each time you pay a deposit at the Universal Bank and don't see a return immediately, realise that at least 138 times you made your deposit in interest. Everything you give out must return to you.

Don't make the mistake of trying to decide when and how your goodwill returns to you, but know that your goodwill comes to you in countless ways if you deposit in the Universal Bank. Often your abundance is quite easy to manifest. Occasionally, in unexpected ways, the goodwill comes to you. Know that it's there.

Chapter 11: Words that Create Results at a Faster Pace

"Words can be like X-rays if you use them properly, they'll go through anything. You read, and you're pierced." - Aldous Huxley

---

11.1. Your Conscious Mind Creates Result

The purpose of this exercise is to replace a set of false beliefs with facts. The unconscious mind wants to reflect on what was offered. The mind and the unconscious mind are called the synthesis of consciousness.

In the end, all we live with is the result of a cause that we have begun. Action and reaction, sowing and harvesting are always present. The value of consciousness must be acknowledged. Techniques can always be taught, but a knowledge of good thinking must be established.

I gave a sales management course to a company in a big city. I explained at the beginning that I would not be teaching them marketing mechanics. They had taken a number of courses. I said I would advise them to build a model of consciousness to establish an inner action or a mental strategy that would allow them to effortlessly sell without being deceptive. A few weeks after the end of the course, the company I was working with announced a 40-percent increase in sales and a significant increase in production for all those involved. They agreed that this kind of training was most helpful because they learned to deal with cause rather than effect.

An example would be if you stood at your front door and looked at the house number directly across the street. You can see that the number on the house is very distinctive when you concentrate on it. But you could be aware of other things on either side of the house even if you look at it without moving your eyes. The other items get more complicated as they move to the right or left of the amount of the house that is the subject. Let's look at how it applies to the cycle of learning. Your core awareness and marginal awareness are like your core vision and marginal sight. There are things you are painfully aware of in your consciousness.

This is your dominant thought. There are things that you are vaguely aware of in your limited consciousness. The marginal thoughts do not control your behaviour, even if they are negative. Your core consciousness or your dominant thoughts govern your actions and your life. You tend to attract the things you love, fear, or constantly expect, that is, the things you hold in your central consciousness.

Anything that prevents my wish from coming to fruition I am willing to give up. I am encouraged and compelled to take steps to foster this intention in all respects. And so it is.

This method is deliberately designed to produce the best results because it is based on the Creative Theory of the mind. Take the time to use it and your ability to produce performance will be increased. You will become more and more aware of the power of your word.

Chapter 12: Think Positive, Identify Your Problems and Achieve Success

---

"Instead of worrying about what you cannot control, shift your energy to what you can create." -
Roy T. Bennett

Don't be afraid if you don't know what to do. You will start to know what to do when you stop resisting the unknown. Search for your own solution whenever you have a problem or a crisis. Don't tell others about it. Through spreading it around, you dilute the severity of the issue, and you dilute the strength and awareness to eradicate it.

The next time you're in a stressful situation, do something completely new. Remember how your mind anxiously seeks an answer, relief and reassurance in the first place. Do something else, and you will be surprised by the new solutions that your intuition will show.

12.1. Identify the Problem and its Solution to Bring about the Change

Do not attempt to solve problems using your memories or previous experiences. You've attempted to solve the problem before by using outdated logic and reasoning. If you knew how to solve the problem already it would have been solved!

When a person says he or she is having a problem, it usually involves a deeper problem. The deeper issue is rarely mentioned, partly because they don't know and partly because they don't agree.

A dilemma cannot be solved if the mind is panicky. It usually turns to the wrong solution, and we continue to go in circles. If you are not in a panic to find a solution, you will be shown the right one. You can move the needle in a variety of wrong directions by shaking a compass. The arrow settles down to the correct and normal direction when you stop moving it around. This is an excellent lesson in solving problems.

You might say, "I understand, but in my case it is different. They intensified my grief. They did it to me." Unfortunately, you give up the power to change if you keep blaming others. Responsibility for the quality of your life is yours.

12.2. Self-reliance over Emotional Dependency

Instead of self-reliance, most of us practice mental dependency. "If you agree with me, and if I am able to duplicate your beliefs and values, I will gain your approval." The decision we make is, "You take care of me, you nurture me, and I will do what you want." It is a terrifying sense to be in a place where you know that your life is dependent on the good nature of another person.

The need to be right and the need to get validation results in psychological dependence. It stems from our need to be emotionally dependent so that we feel loved and cared for. This finding is important since it means that nothing else can give you true self-worth beyond yourself.

Your life is for no one but you, except you give away your power. People will try to control your life when you give your power away. You will be convinced of their knowledge.

When we want something from another person, like love, security, approval, recognition or agreement; tension arises. The expectation is that this individual will accomplish our needs for us.

The secret for a successful life is to get to know yourself. You don't have to look for love from others when you learn to love yourself. You can be more caring instead of looking for love. You can't be taken advantage of if you don't expect anything, because there is no way that anyone can manipulate you. Some people will have difficulties with you if you do not want anything from them, because they cannot control you. But this is the real way of self-reliance and psychological independence.

Adjustment of the Mental State

Most studies show that no one is too old or too young for their views, ideas, principles and pictures to change. You can actually change anything very easily about yourself. You just have to give up the illusion that it takes a long time to change.

Most of us value our television sets differently than our own views.

If our TV needs to be adjusted, we adjust it to make a clearer view. Most of us require daily change and reorganisation. This is what a creative person has to do occasionally. You can tell a person a hundred times that he has to change his views, but until that person tells himself the same thing, nothing will happen.

Be mindful if you have anxiety. Don't run away from it. We are most likely to ignore or suppress this sensation. It can be reduced to manageable proportions if you stop running away from it and face it.

Courage is merely the will to be afraid and to act

There is a line between fear and excitement. You will drive anxiety over the line to excitement if you don't allow the anxiety to stop you. But don't wait until fear becomes panic. You will be very rewarded if you have the confidence to accept your fear, rather than fleeing. It will open up new possibilities and resources for you to share your unlimited potential.

12.3. Say No to Fear of Uncertainty

Don't be afraid of fear. You can have 1,000 fears or not a single fear. You will be open to new ideas, which greatly improves your life when you give up your fear of uncertainty.

12.4. Staying Focused, Knowing your Desire – Path of Success

Do you say, "It's a wonderful day, and I feel great?" Attitudes and conviction have everything to do with it.

They say, "I tried. Heaven knows I tried! But why is something that I'm doing failing?" And then they think," I'm going to try again," but that isn't working either. Why does it not work?

It does not work because the condition of faith has not been established, which will enable them to go where they want to go. They don't trust where they were going. Rather, they concentrate on where they don't want to go. This brings us to a major question: What is your ultimate goal? What do you really want?

Now, pause for a minute. There is no way for you to continue your journey if you cannot answer this question.

The solution is to find out exactly what you want and what you want to do.

How would you explain what your life is like? What are you interested in? If you can answer this honestly, then you're at a good start. Don't put yourself down if the life you really want hasn't been lived. Everything you have done in the past has nothing to do with what you want to do now. Respect the life you led, even if you want to change it.

Someone asked me once what I felt was one of a person's most destructive behaviours. There are many ways of serious self-destruction, but I must say that blind obedience is at the height of the list. To me, it encourages people to do things without thought — the most dangerous thing in the world. In Nazi Germany, millions of Jews were killed with that mentality. The world needs people who challenge and think for themselves more than anything else.

Don't challenge your wishes. The only way you will ever learn if something is right is to experience it. You will find out in time if it is not the right thing. You can then make changes. Life is a corrective cycle. Nonetheless, many people are afraid to make mistakes and are not willing to correct them, so they never get there.

12.5. Say No to Fear of Change

Why haven't we created exactly the kind of life we want to have? We are conditioned to worry about change. We would rather be consistently miserable than take a chance for fear of losing joy and fulfilment. We are always programmed to seek safety and security, and also to fear the unknown. Decision-making teaches you something. Don't get caught in the middle of the pendulum between "yes" and "no" or swing back and forth between "yes" and "no."

Change means addressing the unfamiliar. It consists of moving from the known to the unknown and involves risk. How would you feel if you changed your job today, to one with a higher wage, more opportunities for growth, and better working conditions? You might have some doubt, fear, or insecurity about the change. Even if the shift is good, people can be nervous. It's completely normal.

12.6. Difference between Successful and Unsuccessful People

How successful people manage change is the difference between successful and unsuccessful people. Successful individuals also have anxiety, but they are not immobilised, unlike unsuccessful people.

Successful people are still nervous but turn to innovation. You may know the "Peter Principle," where each of us eventually reaches our failure point and then remains stuck because they are unable to continue. People can remain stuck because of fear of change and refusal to reassess and reprogram to adapt. The Peter Principle states we have limited capacity. But the truth is that due to our fear of change, we stop developing our abilities.

What you have been advised to do is reflect on what isn't, what ought to be, and what might have been. We are brought up with a value system that says that we should assess ourselves continuously, measure ourselves and see whether we are "good." We are judged so rigorously that, because we are afraid to make mistakes, we stop bringing results.

We were taught to be afraid of the unknown and so, instead of focusing on what is, we continue to be worried about what might happens two weeks from now. But the fact is, there will always be the unknown, no matter what you do.

Chapter 13: The Amazing 7 Growth Hacks

"Don't go through life, grow through life." - Eric Butterworth

If you are not where you really want to be, there's likely something in the background that is holding you back. Can you imagine what it is? Hint: It has the power to transform your life completely–you have a choice. It's positive (or negative). It's the MINDSET!

Your thoughts drip into every area of your life and can change your job, your career, your mind, your relationship and your life in general. That is why, in order to shift your outlook and push you more positive towards life, I dig into my top 7 mind-set hacks.

Hack 1 - Become Aware Of Your Thoughts

Your thoughts are all about you. It is important to look closely at your feelings, as we often aren't aware of what we think. The more you watch over your emotions, the more you realise that you are fully controlled by them.

Hack 2 - Reframe Your Thoughts Using The Ctfar Model

The CTFAR Model is the idea that thoughts create feelings, feelings create your behaviours and ultimately your outcomes. You can take power back in your life by seeing the world in that way. Instead of the passenger, you are the driver of your life.

The CTFAR Model

1. **Circumstances**: are neutral.
2. **Thoughts:** are optional.
3. **Feelings**: what are the feelings associated with these thoughts?
4. **Action**: how do those feelings determines the action we take?
5. **Result**: what is the result caused by the action?

For example, you may experience a thought with mixed feelings: anger and rage generate varying feelings.

You can use the CTFAR model to create different paths, each ending with different results. By including all your path possibilities, you will also expose unwanted thought patterns. Once you decide on the one that arrives at the best outcome and brings the most joy, utilise that model.

To create your various models, use sticky notes on a wall so that you can visualise the varying thoughts and feelings. This is a very practical method you can use to adjust, thoughts, feelings and actions, giving you a clear insight into your thoughts, and the best way to proceed.

Hack 3 - Positive Affirmations

It goes without saying that if you repeat something enough, you will start to believe it.

There are so many affirmations I love to use every day, but here is one of my favourites: I control my life, my life doesn't control me. You must envision your future as you want it. By doing so, you instinctively identify with your future and get closer every day to bring it.

Hack 4 - Get Rid Of Limiting Words

The self-talk represents your values, and anything you think will ultimately become the outcome in your life. Therefore, modifying your vocabulary to match your thought is so important. I would advise you to start by eliminating specific words like "can't," "don't," "unable, "never". People who succeed are thinking, "I can do XYZ, I will do XYZ, and I'll get it done today." Remove yourself from your feelings and ask what you think. Adjust your language to support the person you want to be. Please ask yourself (see below) powerful questions that will bring you closer to your future.

Hack 5 - Ask Yourself Questions

If you ask negative questions, then negative answers will be received; but if you ask positive questions, then positive answer will be given. So, if you're wondering "Why am I always poor?" The brain will only focus on reasons that you are poor. But, when you ask, "How can I earn more money?" The brain comes with ideas on how to make more money for you. Here you can ask yourself some big questions:

- What can I do today to get me closer to my goals?
- In my business, how can I make more money?
- Who do I want to be in the future?
- How would I think, behave and feel if I was the person that I want to be?
- To achieve my goals, what do I need to know?
- What do I still don't know?
- If I could believe something, what would I believe?

Asking these questions can help you dive deeper into answers that produce the most results.

Hack 6 - Add "No Matter What" To Your Thought Process

This hack is a mentality I like to use when I'm not motivated to deal with my most difficult task. Essentially, if I have anything important to do, but I sense some pressure, I assure myself that I will achieve the mission. For instance, I would tell myself that I no matter what, I need to write 15 blog posts in a day or organise my closet. I'm a person who is going to do all I can to get what I want if I want it bad enough.

Hack 7 - Create An Alter Ego For Yourself

I like to use this hack most of all! It is based on Todd Herman's book *The Alter Ego Effect*. Do you feel like you want something in your life, but then feel like you don't? Does your own personality make you stand still in your own way and take no opportunity?

Here is a convenient way to create an alter ego. To begin with, think of the person you would like to be who has the results you want. Next, create an alter ego of the ideal person and pretend to be it until you really become it.

I have altered egos for various areas of my life, whether it is for company or health purposes. I offer myself the freedom to make myself stronger and bolder. You continue to adopt the habits and values by practising being your alter ego.

Now go back to the start of this book and utilise the bonus change hacks mentioned at the beginning. These 3 extra change hacks will help solidify your progress.

Final Thoughts

If you use these hacks, they will change your mindset from scarcity to abundance, so you can take away any restrictive confidence that holds you back and finally build the life of which you have dreamt!

I had a lot of convictions that I couldn't understand, and they kept me behind for years. I lacked the strength and insight to move forward with faith in my life until I did these activities and worked on my attitude every day. I promise you can do the same! My recommendation is to incorporate these separately, and before you know it, you will change profoundly!

Conclusion

Positive thinking is a healing agent for not just your body, but for your soul too, therefore initiating a process of self-improvement ultimately embarking on a path of success followed by achieving it. According to recent research "happy people" are more pleased with their work and show more independence.

Moreover, they perform best and receive more support from their colleagues than their less happy peers. Ultimately, the odds of positive people becoming unemployed are lower, their mentally safer, and they are likely to live longer. And the argument about happiness and jobs goes back a long way in history.

The ancient Greek philosopher Galen said that work was "nature's physician," key to the happiness of humans.

"Power Naps" can improve right-brain activities that will lead to opportunities when people are optimistic at work because they are more active and resilient. The book explicitly covered how to learn to think positively, what are the factors that govern positive thinking and how a positive mindset makes it easier to achieve a positive attitude thereby ensuring success.

Success is beyond positive thinking but definitely the outcome of it. You always start with the basics that later translate into bigger achievements. Positive thinking is the first step to any change in life. A positive attitude is achieved when even your subconscious is in harmony with your conscious state of mind with which you intentionally instil a habit of positive thinking.

All this ultimately helps you to create your own reality. When you are aware of your capabilities, only then you can subjugate all the fears of change and uncertainty. Big achievements are marked by a series of big and small mistakes. Nothing goes perfect all along the way. Accept the very essence of every successful journey and keep on the path consistently with a changing pace. As nothing is attained at a steady pace, there are highs there are lows, what matters at the end of the day is staying focused. Growth, no matter how small, is growth - and every step towards it counts. That is how you become successful with a positive mindset.

To learn more about instilling better habits see our book How To Change Habits in 30 days: 7 Hacks

To learn more about coaching and mindset training see our website: www.MindsetMastership.com

- Abbas, Raja, Darr, & Bouckenooghe. (2012). *Teacher's Turnover Intentions: Examining the Impact of Motivation and Organizational Commitment.* March 21, 2020. Available at https://www.researchgate.net/publication/308779545_Teacher's_Turnover_Intentions_Examining_the_Impact_of_Motivation_and_Organizational_Commitment

- Rick Snyder. (2002). *Hope Theory: Rainbows in the Mind.* 21, 2020. Available at: https://www.jstor.org/stable/1448867?seq=1

- Fred Luthans. (2011). *Organizational Behavior An Evidence-Based Approach 12 Edition.* March 21, 2020. Available at: https://bdpad.files.wordpress.com/2015/05/fred-luthans-organizational-behavior-_-an-evidence-based-approach-twelfth-edition-mcgraw-hill_irwin-2010.pdf

- Judge, T. and Watanabe, S. (1993). *Another Look at the Job Satisfaction-Life Satisfaction Relationship.* March 21, 2020. Available at https://psycnet.apa.org/record/1994-17491-001

- Lorenz, Beer, Pütz, & Heinitz. (2016). *Measuring Psychological Capital: Construction and Validation of the Compound PsyCap Scale (CPC-12)* March 21, 2020. Available at: https://journals.plos.org/plosone/article?id=10.1371/journal.pone.0152892

- Bandura, A. (1997). *Self-efficacy: The Exercise of Control.* March 21, 2020. Available at: https://psycnet.apa.org/record/1997-08589-000

- Reivich, K., & Shatté, A. (2002). *Resilience Factor: 7 Essential Skills for Overciming Life's Inevitable Obstacles.* March 21, 2020. *The* Available at: https://psycnet.apa.org/record/2002-18688-000

Printed in Great Britain
by Amazon